Enchanted

About the Author

Shivangi Gajwani Jain is a doctor by profession and a poet and prose writer by choice. Born in the family of doctors in 1981, she graduated in dentistry from Nair Hospital Dental College, Mumbai and did her post-graduation in prosthodontics from A.B.S.M.I.D.S, Mangalore.

Recipient of International College of Dentists Merit Award in the year 2003, Dr. Shivangi is presently a practising clinician in Mumbai.

Enchanted

A Little Magic in Our Lives

Dr. Shivangi Gajwani Jain

Mind Melodies

New Delhi

First published 2009

Published by
Mind Melodies
An imprint of *Readworthy Publications (P) Ltd.*

Regd. Off.: A-18, Mohan Garden
Near Nawada Metro Station
New Delhi – 110 059 (India)
Phone: 011-2537 1324
Fax: +91-11-2537 1323

Branch: 4735/22, Prakash Deep
Building, Ground Floor,
Ansari Road, Daryaganj
New Delhi – 110 002
Phone: 011-43549197
Fax: +91-11-23243060

Email: info@mindmelodies.com Web: www.mindmelodies.com

Cataloging in Publication Data– DK
Courtesy: D.K. Agencies (P) Ltd. <docinfo@dkagencies.com>

Jain, Shivangi Gajwani, 1981-
Enchanted : a little magic in our lives / Shivangi Gajwani Jain.
p. cm.
Poems.
ISBN 13: 978-81-908020-4-8 ISBN 10: 81-908020-4-6
1. Indic poetry (English) 2. Life--Poetry. I. Title.

DDC 821.92 22

Printed at Salasar Imaging Systems, Delhi - 35

Life only is, or death is life disguised, -Life, a short death until by Life we are surprised.

Sri Aurobindo

Contents

	Acknowledgements	10
	Note on the texts	11
	Prologue	13
1.	Sonnet by the Sea	15
2.	You	17
3.	Vande Maatram	19
4.	Contentment	21
5.	Cold Reality	23
	Quotes by Khalil Gibran	
6.	Rhymes and Rhythms	27
7.	As Down a Flower	29
8.	A Strange Meeting	31
	Quotes by: Robert Frost	
9.	Time Speaks	35
10.	Oh Fair Lady	37
11.	A Soldier Lives	39
12.	The Reflection	41
13.	Soul still Lives	43
	Quotes by: Mahatma Gandhi	
14.	A Hundred Dawns and Setting Suns	47
	Quotes by: Harvey Mackay	
15.	Unspoken Truth	51
16.	Against the Devil's Hands	53
17.	My Own Grave	55
	Quotes by: Tennyson	
	Quotes by: Dr. Kamal Kishore	
18.	Life's Game Plan	59

19. An Old Metal Pen 61
20. Time Goes by 63
21. An Old Man's Wisdom 65
Quotes by: Sri Aurobindo
22. Smile Please 69
23. Shadows of the Past 71
Quotes by: Plato
24. Can You Read My Mind! 75
25. Happiness has no Memory 77
26. The Wonder 79
27. A Song is Made 81
28. I Believe 83
Quotes by: Buddha
29. Desire 87
30. Hope of a New Way of Life 89
Quotes by: Oscar Wilde
31. Face of Fear 93
32. Until 95
33. A Poet's Perspective 99
Quotes by: Theodore Roethke
34. My Magic Room 103
Quotes by: Lyman Frank Baum
35. Death of Fireflies 107
36. God's Words 111
37. I, For You 113
38. His Sonnets and Prose 115
39. As I Sleep 117
Quotes by: W. H. Auden

Dedication

This collection of poems is dedicated to my Father

Dr. Rajesh Gajwani,

Without whom this book would not have been possible.

Acknowledgements

Special thanks to all those who have helped in the shaping of my ideas, encouraged me to think big andmost of all through all stages of my life believed in meand my dreams.

My family has encouraged me from day one. I hadnothing but a few pages full of ideas and my perspectiveabout life in the subtle form of poetry. As I faced manyclosed doors, they offered me love, unforgettable supportand most importantly they believed in my book. I amblessed to have such a wonderful family who stood by mein turbulent times...

To my Nanaji Dr. Kamal Kishore, who inspired me and taught me that, there is always time to read and write inone's busy schedule. My Nani Uma Kishore for her love and my Mother Dr. Madhu Gajwani for her encouraging words and tremendous patience. My Sister Astha, who spent hours together to make my book esthetic and presentable for the reader's consumption.

To Ranjan Jain, a friend and father-in-law, who reviewed my work and Poonam Jain, my mother-in-law who has always shown faith in my writing. My Husband Prateek, who has filled my life with happiness.

My publishers Readworthy Publications, who have given me a platform to present my dreams to the people of India. I would like to acknowledge the efforts put in by Mr. Shalaj Mittal, Director, Readworthy Publications, and special thanks for his immense patience. God, who continues to look after me despite my flaws.

Note on the texts

This book contains all my poems, composed within a span of ten years, with the exception of poems written solely as experiments, poems written as parodies and incomplete or fragmentary poems. Language used is basic, simple English to emphasize on the meaning and the thought behind each one of my writings. Most of the poems included are "lyrical" in the technical sense: they are short and express my personal thoughts and feelings.

Prologue

Every morning, like most of us I rise with the burden of daily chores and a sense of monotony of routine. Like each one of us, I wait for the weekends to relax and unwind. But I specially long for those days when a thought enters my mind and fills my complete being with vigor. As I pour this energy on a piece of paper, I feel deep love and it forms a nexus between my soul and the heaven above, making each moment celestial: its pure magic!

Any abstract thought taking refuge of words, creates harmony in the form of my poems.

I believe: To express harmony, of all things Simplicity is the best.

1

Sonnet by the Sea

A silver raft floats afar,
Bathed in a pale blue glow..
It drifts in the infinite ocean,
Slowly dancing with the flow.

It shimmers in the faint night,
Smiling at the crescent above..
Revealing the honest beauty of nature,
It swings with the spirit of love.

2

You

There's a new aura around me,
Which i have never felt before..
Something that leaves me dreaming,
And always waiting for more.

There's change in my world around,
Special, beautiful and one of a kind..
Is it you who has touched my heart,
Or is it a mirage of my mind.

3

Vande Maatram

Today is the day of rising,
Rising of a nation as whole..
We begin to walk the untrodden path,
The path to freedom: our great goal.

We prepare to leap over the last brow,
Our heads held high with pride..
Millions of hearts beat as one,
As we stride with God as our guide.

Vande Maatram..Vande Maatram,
Simple words adorn our lips..
Words spoken to last forever,
Touch our souls with divine bliss.

4

Contentment

I wake up every morning,
To the sounds of village bell..
I see the crimson ball rising,
Weaving colours in a magical spell.

I gather my hammyed down tools,
To start my daily chores..
I need to earn a few pennies,
Five or six or some more.

I call out to my woman,
As she comes to say good bye..
Holds my face in her hands,
And kisses me with a sigh.

Draped in an old weathered dress,
There stands my lovely bride..
I ask her if she wants anything,
She smiles as she hides.

I feel immense gratitude,
As i pray to the heavens above..
What more could one want,
Hard work and true love

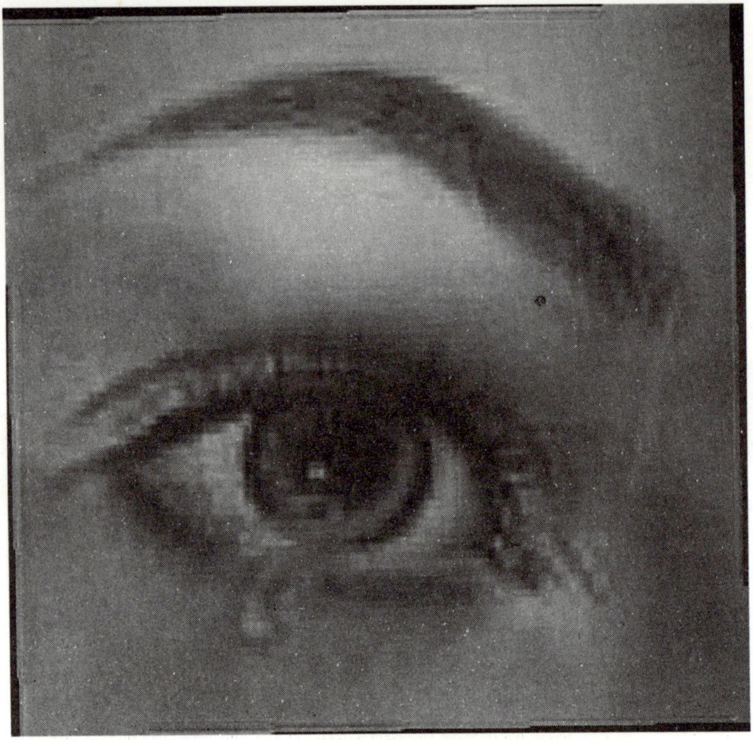

5

Cold Reality

As doors close,
I stand alone..
With a sense of despair,
And a heart of stone.

As a lone tear,
Slowly trickles down..
I bow to my fate,
And so falls my crown.

Khalil Gibran

"...the timeless in you is aware of life's timelessness, And knows that yesterday is but to-day's memory and to-morrow is to-day's dream."

"In God's field of Beauty, at the edge of the stream of life, I was imprisoned in the cage of laws made by man."

"And think not you can direct the course of love, for love, if it finds you worthy, directs your course."

"Love possesses not nor would it be possessed; For love is sufficient unto love. When you love you should not say, "God is in my heart," but rather, I am in the heart of God."

"Your children are not your children. They are the sons and daughters of Life's longing for itself...
You may house their bodies but not their souls, for their souls dwell in the house of tomorrow, which you cannot visit, not even in your dreams."

"You talk when you cease to be at peace with your thoughts. And when you can no longer dwell in the solitude of your heart you live in your lips, and sound is a diversion and a pastime
For thought is a bird of space, that in a cage of words may indeed unfold its wings but can not fly."

"It is so unusual for people to realize that love means being individuals who choose to stay together while remaining individuals."

6

Rhymes and Rhythms

There's sweet music that softer falls,
Than petals from blown roses on the grass,
Music that gentlier on the spirit lies,
Than tired eyelids upon tired eyes.
It lingers in my mind, each moment of every day,

It touches my heart, my soul in every way,
It creates rhythm in my each breath,
Causing turmoil of feelings underneath.
And i rise to dance on my own,
Like the waves which rise to touch the moon. .

7

As Dawn a Flower

I know I can't keep you now,
As its time for you to go..
Suns peeking from above the mountains,
Warming my bed with a secret glow.

Promise me you will come again,
At night in the same loving way..
Embracing me in a tender hug,
Driving all my fears away.

You have never made me feel alone,
In the dark nights so to say..
Dreams, oh Dreams thank you,
For always coming my way

8

A Strange Meeting

As i try to smile
A Ghost of a grin creeps on to my face,
Terror stricken i try again
My lips twitch but the grin stays.

I close my eyes obliterating my view
Embracing this darkness of a different kind,
Just as relief starts to melt my defenses
I see an unfocused image in my mind.

A strange being floating in thin air
Dark robes swaying on its own accord,
An unpleasant aura surrounds its form
Inhuman, black, large and broad.

It comes to a sudden halt
As i struggle to keep pace,
Causing a deathly stillness around
Bearing me down with quiet menace.

My eyes focus on its back
Willing it to turn around,
I try to formulate words
Can't articulate even a single sound.

As this dark shadow decides to turn
I sway on my feet with the impact given,
Breathing hard to combat this shock
And the darkness threatening to engulf my vision.

This ghostly pale face i know
Saw it in the mirror before i closed my eyes,
Staring again from the back of my mind
My heart pains, my soul cries.

Slowly as i open my unsure eyes
Revealing what i was trying to hide,
Tears shimmer as i stare at my face
It was strange meeting my dark side...

Robert Frost

"A poet never takes notes. You never take notes in a love affair."

"But I have promises to keep, and miles to go before I sleep, and miles to go before I sleep.
Forgive, O Lord, my little jokes on Thee, and I'll forgive Thy great big joke on me."

"In three words I can sum up everything I've learned about life: it goes on".

"Two roads diverged in a wood and I - I took the one less traveled by, and that has made all the difference."

"Thinking isn't agreeing or disagreeing. That's voting."

"To be a poet is a condition, not a profession."

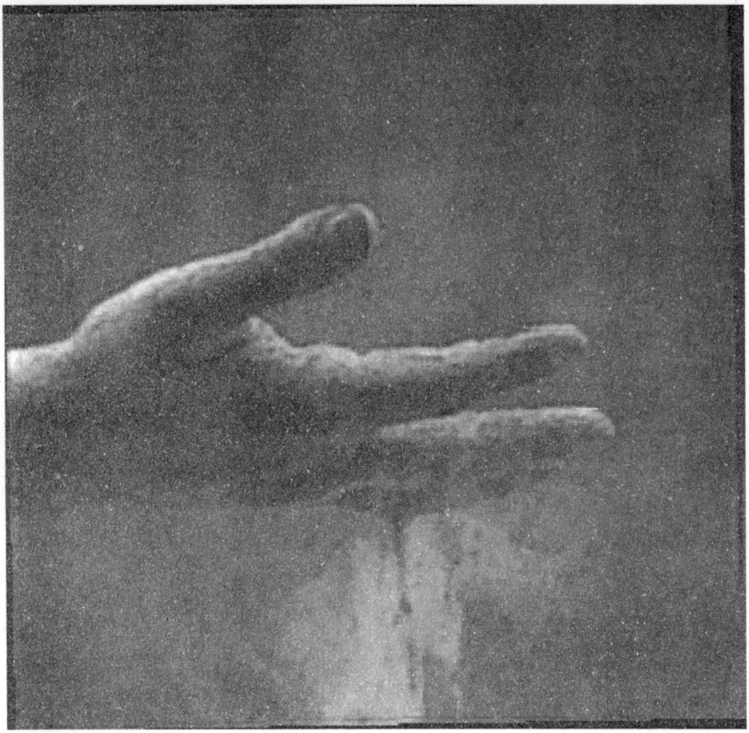

9

Time Speaks

Life goes on,
Stops for no one.
I want to keep pace,
So i try to run.

I want to hold on,
It slips from my hand.
Like the drops of water,
Or the grains of sand.

10

Oh Fair Lady

Smile smile
Oh fair lady,
For it will melt my heart
And drive me crazy.

It is not your skin
It is not your eyes,
It is your heart
Where my love lies.

It is your power
Which turns the world around,
Your presence brings music
Without a single sound.

You are the one
And i know its true,
Words i have shuddered to say
I want to say to you.

Believe it or not
"i love you"

11

A Soldier Lives

Many soldiers died in a war,
This is what morning newspapers say..
Neither waited for a natural death,
Nor for their hair to gray.

Bullets struck each one of them,
As they fell for their country..
Yes, they were her true sons,
Who lived to see their mother free.

And now as they are no more,
Their bodies lay buried in their mother's chest..
On every tomb a message is written,
For those who proved to be the best.

Epitaph:
"You nourished me from the day of my birth,
And i lived on your tender heart..
Now you have accepted me as one with you,
From this moment we will never part."

12

The Reflection

I lie in my bed and i wait,
Every night for the morning sunshine,
As i see the sun rising,
I wait for something divine.

As i look in the mirror,
I blush but try to hide,
Cause it stirs something deep down,
I guess the woman inside.

13

Soul still Lives

A plant endures the chilly winds of autumn,
Covered by snowflakes, it stays forgotten.

Hoping against hope for something divine,
For the snow to melt and sun to shine.

Shudders when its blood feels cold,
Stands alone though small, tiny still so bold.

Counting days and nights all in vain,
Waiting forever it bears the pain.

Seconds turn into minutes, minutes into hours and days,
It stands there listening to the winds of change.

One fine morning when it rises from its slumber,
Gazes around at its new world in wonder.

There's an interplay of colour and light,
Fills its little heart with awe and delight.

As the sunrays give it warmth inside,
It flutters its leaves and stands with pride.

As the world is bathed in a golden river,
It grows and fills with beauty and vigor.

A little shy bud opens its eyes,
Peeps through its sepals and smiles.

Beauty of life touches it to the core,
It smiles at you, wants nothing more.

As the clock chimes, time goes by,
It shrivels and prepares to die.

This story is old, which i have told,
Its body is one with sun and rays of gold.

But the soul still lives, is no ones slave,
In the tiny seed buried near its grave...

Mahatma Gandhi

"A small body of determined spirits fired by an unquenchable faith in their mission can alter the course of history."

"You must be the change you wish to see in the world."

"A principle is the expression of perfection, and as imperfect beings like us cannot practice perfection, we devise every moment limits of its compromise in practice."

"In the attitude of silence the soul finds the path in a clearer light, and what is elusive and deceptive resolves itself into crystal clearness. Our life is a long and arduous quest after Truth."

"Whatever you do will be insignificant, but it is very important that you do it."

"Happiness is when what you think, what you say, and what you do are in harmony."

"You don't have to burn books to destroy a culture. Just get people to stop reading them".

14

A Hundred Dawns and Setting Suns

I dream of angels in heaven,
Smiling at our earth and its men.

Walking amongst wisps of silver cloud,
Singing the hymns of love clear and loud.

I see colours merging in flawless divinity,
A rainbow blossoms flowing towards infinity.

Golden and silver, Orange and red sun's rays,
Rising and falling, gleaming in wondrous ways.

As i stir awake and open my eyes,
I hit reality, my heart cries.

Men are slaves of their own mind,
Honesty, trust, love they have left behind.

Fires of hell aired by human spite,
As i shiver in the endless cold night.

My fellow beings in an ardour to win,
Are making friends with lust and sin.

I close my tired eyes once again,
Desperate to wipe off this image of man.

Praying to God to give me a chance,
To wake up anew from this trance.

From the depths of my being i yearn,
To see the flame of eternal truth burn.

I desire my pristine dream come true,
A new me, A new you!!

Harvey Mackay

"Time is free, but it's priceless. You can't own it, but you can use it. You can't keep it, but you can spend it. Once you've lost it you can never get it back."

"Many people may listen, but few people actually hear"

"Find something you love to do and you'll never have to work a day in your life."

"Optimists are right. So are pessimists. It's up to you to choose which you will be."

15

Unspoken Truth

We live our life,
For many years on end,
Believing in its immortality,
Living only in present.

It comes in our nature,
Not to accept death,
Leaving things for tomorrow,
Breathing our very last breath.

16

Against the Devil's Hands

A raging storm is brewing,
Screaming, howling and growling.

Thundering with all its might,
Splashing fire the whole night.

Scary, dark, black cloud's curtain,
Looming death feels so certain.

Yet we sleep unknowing,
Of the brutal chaos growing.

Thanks to our trusted friend,
Holding forte years on end.

Rocking violently on its hinges,
Bearing pain as it flinches.

Our old closed door stands,
Even against the devil's hands.

17

My Own Grave

I lost him in war,
Who taught me to live,
Once again deep silence,
My heart feels still.

Sparkling tears glittering,
At the corner of my eye,
Shining like diamonds,
They refuse to run by.

Even as I burn,
Cold spreads inside,
Senses leave senses,
Drop by drop I bleed.

Body turns into ashes,
His soul lives on,
I die entirely. In earnest,
Living with in my own.

Tennyson

"Best words for your thoughts are prose,
Best order for your words is poetry".

"Essence of thought must come on the surface of words.."

"Dreams are true while they last, and do we not live in dreams?"

"God's finger touched him, and he slept."

Dr. Kamal Kishore

"Life is present in sand and stone,
As it is present the dead and gone".

"Life is nothing but energy. It is omnipresent and omnipotent. It is present in the living. It is present in the corpse. While living it is moving and active, while corpse it disseminates into five fundamentals and offers them to the universe"

"The Supreme entity: The light of the sun that illuminates the whole world, the light that is moon and fire, know it to be mine. I dwell in the heart of all living beings and from me develop the memory, knowledge and ability to set aside all doubts."

"The innate inclination of supreme sacrifice present in everybody is Lord himself"

18

Life's Game Plan

Time goes on smoothly,
But as I start to smile..
Always something happens,
And shatters my simple life.

As I see a lovely dream,
It is followed by a nightmare..
I feel lost in uncertainty,
As nothing seems fair.

I stand deathly still,
Looking at the broken pieces..
Holding back my unshed tears,
Learning from what life teaches

I walk slowly towards them,
Gathering them in my hand..
Carrying them to that corner,
Where alone I stand.

I figure out life's game plan,
As I wait in that dark corner..
Life breaks as it heals,
Till your soul becomes stronger.

19

An Old Metal Pen

An old metal pen,
Lifeless as it seems,
Hiding in its heart,
A thousand unsaid dreams.

The dead, cold pen,
As I touch with my finger,
Loses its deathly stillness,
Awakens from its slumber.

As I take a strong grip,
Hold it firmly in my hand,
It strikes fire from words,
Moves like a magic wand.

20

Time Goes by..

Things happen,
Time goes by...

It never stops,
It is there to fly.
Even if I hold it,
However hard I try.

Things happen,
Time goes by...

21

An Old Man's Wisdom

Life! Here i am at your doorstep,
What can you give me?

LIFE: "I have mountains and valleys,
Covered in greens, studded with flowers..
Deep oceans with hidden secrets,
Treasures which one dreams from far.

My fresh cool breath riding on winds,
Morning mist penetrated by golden red rays..
Shimmering full moon smiling in its beauty,
Silvery waves dancing in different ways.

Old Man!I have so much to give,
What do you want?"

OLD MAN: Life, this is not true,
Listen to me..
Open your eyes,
And try to see, what i see.

"I see mountains and valleys,
Ugly, gray scattered with rotting trees..
Black ocean with hidden death,
Shiny stones which do not mean a thing to me.

Sunrays obscured by the morning smog,
Winds blinded by factory smoke, sighing..
Moon basking in its scarred glory,
Screaming waves failing, falling and dying."

Life, Is this all you have?

"Why you stand so tall and proud,
I can see you bent and old..
Do not pretend, as I know the truth,
And all the lies, which you hold.

When i was young, I was full of vigor,
Now i am old and spent and so are you..
You have nothing more and are tired like me,
My time has come and i am through."
Dear life..
Thank you for standing by my side,
As i close my eyes to you i confide..
Let me go and rest in peace
As i am tired of life itself.

Sri Aurobindo

"The Spirit shall look out through Matter's gaze
And Matter shall reveal the Spirit's face.
Then man and superman shall be at one
And all the earth become a single life."

"Arise, transcend thyself. Thou art man and the whole nature of man is to become more than himself"

A thought is an arrow shot at the truth; it can hit a point , but not cover the whole target. But the archer is too well satisfied with his success to ask anything farther.

India of the ages is not dead nor has she spoken her last creative word; she lives and has still something to do for herself and the humans.

22

Smile Please

Smile Please,
Cause it makes my heart smile..

That look on your face,
Yes, it follows me at every place.
Your beautiful eyes looking at me,
As if saying a silent plea.

Your hair tied in a careless knot,
Gives me a look, which says a lot.
As the wind blows over a lonely river,
You give a sigh and your lips quiver.

What is it that you want to hide,
Tell me, i promise to be on your side.
Why you always give me that searching look,
As if you can read me like an open book.

Don't feel scared and insecure,
Cause i love you and my heart is pure.
Look into my eyes and say i do,
As you are for me and i for you.

Hear the wedding bells for you and me,
And I will love you till eternity.
So Smile please,
Cause it makes my heart smile..

23

Shadows of the Past

A secret glow warmed her face,
As she wore her wedding dress,
Smoothened her long black curls,
Blushed, as she looked at her beautiful self.

This was the day she had been waiting for,
She smiled at her image in the mirror,
Told her self a zillionth time as before,
That he was the one, the only one for her.

She turned around and saw her love,
Opened her arms trying to reach him,
Suddenly the room started to swirl,
Sunshine vanished, lights became dim.

And there she was restless in the bed,
Eyes staring at nothing at all,
Her fists rolled in a painful way,
On her palms were impressions of her nails.

Lips twitched as if wanting something to say,
Her face was covered with cold sweat,
A lone tear trickled down its way,
Bringing Her back to the truth, her fate.

She tried to see blinking her tears away,
The blue eyes of a smiling man,
Her heart contracted in a similar pain,
Which she had experienced time and again.

She came back from her trans,
As something stirred at her side,
Her sense of loss lessened,
As she saw those smiling blue eyes.

God had given her his shadow,
Something for her to survive,
She would never be alone,
For their son had the same blue eyes.

Plato

"At the touch of love everyone becomes a poet."

"Love is the joy of the good, the wonder of the wise, the amazement of the Gods."

"Music is a moral law. It gives soul to the universe, wings to the mind, flight to the imagination, and charm and gaiety to life and to everything."

"Philosophy is the highest music."

"Poetry is nearer to vital truth than history."

"Thinking: the talking of the soul with itself."

"We can easily forgive a child who is afraid of the dark; the real tragedy of life is when men are afraid of the light."

"Wonder is the feeling of the philosopher, and philosophy begins in wonder."

24

Can You Read My Mind!

Your eyes sparkling,
With a shade of fire and ice,
Says much more,
Than words can suffice.

Your smile reaching to your eyes,
Is the home, where my heart lies,
Soothing words which you say to me,
Will stay with me till eternity.

Every loving word you have ever said,
And the unspoken promises made,
Brightens my life with a soft glow,
Do you see it, do you know.

I feel deep love for you,
Can you feel it too,
I have been trying to hide,
But to you I confide.
Today I want you....
......to read my mind.

25

Happiness has no Memory

As I look back,
And I try to see,
One scene follows another,
Happiness has no memory.

But when misery strikes,
It leaves a scar,
Thriving on our memory,
Causing suffering for hours.

Not just hours but days,
It stays for years on end,
Giving us pitiful company,
Pretending to be our friend.

Our life is full of events,
Some mild, some intense,
Happiness survives in moments,
Let us believe in its presence.

In the warmth of sun,
In the air we breathe,
It is omnipresent,
Yet we fail to see.

Rise my fellow beings,
Above the shackles of memory,
Learn to live in the moment,
And let your soul free..

26

The Wonder

As the subtle breeze flows,
Leaves move in a rhythm,
Swaying from side to side,
Dancing from with in..

Early morning sun rises,
Showering orange golden rays,
Dewdrops shimmer like jewels,
Enchanting me in different ways..

The wonder is not the wind,
Not the sun or changing seasons,
The wonder is - my wrinkled eyes,
Allowing me to experience God's creations.

27

A Song is Made..

Left Right Left!
Soldier's marching,
Down the road.
Early morning,
In the cold.

That is the sound,
Echoing in the hills.
Their daily routine,
The morning drill.

Left Right Left!
Left leg follows,
The rhythm of right.
Moving up and down,
Marching in stride.

A voice is heard,
Someone starts to hum.
Rhythm of the march,
Creates a natural strum.

Left Right Left!
A chorus begins,
As a song is made.
Warming their hearts,
Till the song fades..

28

I Believe

You, who do not believe in magic,
Who are busy with the daily grind..
Following the same routine in the usual way,
Yes you, and all of your kind.

Look around you and see,
From the heart, with an open mind..
It is not me, who keeps harping about magic,
I have the whole world by my side.

Our next door neighbor, you know don't you,
She has given birth to a beautiful child..
There's magic as one becomes two,
The divine arrival of a new life.

Every morning as the birds sing,
The radiant sun shines bright..
Every evening it changes colour just for you,
Yellow to orange to red to say good night.

When sunshine meets raindrops,
Seven beautiful colours fill the sky..
Mother earth smiles enchanted,
Can you feel it, please try.

Look at a tiny little bud,
Quiet, closed and mysteriously shy..
And then it opens and gives away its secrets,
When god waves his magic wand high.

Remember that young sweet little thing,
Yes the one who works at the bakery above..
See her blush when the Shepherd arrives,
That is magic!

Magic of Love

Buddha

"No one saves us but ourselves. No one can and no one may. We ourselves must walk the path".

"All that we are is the result of what we have thought. The mind is everything. What we think we become."

"Have compassion for all beings, rich and poor alike; each has their suffering. Some suffer too much, others too little."

"The whole secret of existence is to have no fear. Never fear what will become of you, depend on no one. Only the moment you reject all help are you freed.

29

Desire

Give me what I want.....

For it'll bring tears of pleasure,
My heart will beat faster,
It will make my mind dizzy,
With pure joy and laughter.

My tired eyes will sparkle,
As I will look with awe,
A smile will break on my lips,
And there it'll always stay.

Give me what I want,
And I will not ask again,
I will be content and happy,
As inner peace will remain.

30

Hope of a New Way of Life

In a small far away village,
At the banks of river Ganges,
I lived.. A poor farmer,
Surviving on meager wages.

With each dawn I began,
Ploughing and sowing days on end,
I worked like a mad man,
To yield my infertile land.

With little rice and loads of water,
I started once again,
Starving and still surviving,
My daily chores I began.

Ploughing and sowing, sowing and ploughing,
These were the only tasks I knew,
Till I heard the neighbors talk,
With each word my interest grew.

They spoke of a great man,
Who stood against the British rule,

No guns, knives or pistols,
He fought with a different tool.

He wore colour of peace,
And he taught non-violence,
As his voice touched my soul,
My existence started to make sense.

He rallied vast crowds,
Spoke to him and him and me,
He knew of each of our plight,
Our sorrows he could see.

Hope of a new way of life,
He filled with in me.
World heard the voice of a leader,
His name was Gandhi.

That day I stepped out in open,
As I left my life of misery,
Like thousands of people I decided,
To write my own destiny.

As I marched along side my kin,
To witness a part of history,
Lathis and bullets I accepted,
To die a death of dignity.

Oscar Wilde

" A dreamer is one who can only find his way by moonlight, and his punishment is that he sees the dawn before the rest of the world."

"All that I desire to point out is the general principle that life imitates art far more than art imitates life."

"Most people are other people. Their thoughts are someone else's opinions, their lives a mimicry, their passions a quotation."

"There is no such thing as a moral or an immoral book. Books are well written, or badly written."

"Illusion is the first of all pleasures."

"If one cannot enjoy reading a book over and over again, there is no use in reading it at all."

31

Face of Fear

Rainy night and the lightning was on,
Vast sky and all the stars had gone.

Hiding under the clouds cover,
Making the night as black as ever.

I increased my pace once again,
Holding my cloak I faced the rain.

Noises hushed by the pitter-patter,
Muffed wet silence filled my ears.

Faces loomed from every dark corner,
I walked and walked, as if forever.

Suddenly I stopped with a loud cry,
Waiting for me were those deathly eyes.

Death staring, feeding on my fear,
I sat down for my last prayer.

Opened my eyes on the sound of mew,
I saw death purring against my shoe. .

32

Until..

I see her
kissing her new born baby,
I see him
scolding the elder one..

I see,
me
in front of a mirror.
Trying to see
my real self
The true me.

My vision
is blurred,
by tears..
Oh my tears!

But why?
Don't know.
Missing something?
Guess so.

Something,
I had lost.
Something,
I never had.

I miss her kisses,
His immense eyes,
His scolding,
Where his love lies.

I feel..
alone.
I feel..
unwanted.

Can you understand?
Help me.
Please don't wait,
Adopt me.

If it's too late for me,
don't worry.
Just don't hesitate,
adopt somebody..
..another me.

I hope
you know,
How it feels
to be so.

Because
until yesterday,
I never understood
what they say.

The feeling
of being alone.
The feeling
of being an orphan.
Until…

I saw her
kissing her new born baby,
And him
Scolding the elder one.

33

A Poet's Perspective

Nothingness,
The great impelling force.
Felt alone,
Began praying for more.

God smiled,
Raised his hand.
The space,
Came unto it.

Space sacrificed its energy,
To give birth.
To sun, moon, stars,
And created earth.

Earth felt barren,
Began to cry.
Thus rain started,
Falling from the sky.

Wet and cold,
Earth coughed and sneezed.
Filled with thunder,
Formed wind and breeze.

Five elements,
Stood hand in hand.
In a mysterious way,
They created man.

It all began,
From its source.
A little desire,
And divine force.

One day it will end,
Revert once again,
To lonely nothingness,
Where it all began.

Theodore Roethke

"All lovers live by longing, and endure;
summon a vision and declare it pure"

"I came to love, I came into my own."

"In a dark time, the eye begins to see."

"Time marks us while we are marking time."

"What is madness but nobility of soul at odds with circumstance."

"A lively understandable spirit Once entertained you. It will come again. Be still. Wait."

34

My Magic Room

In nature chaos,
Prevalent everywhere.
World ruthless,
Life not fair.

I do not cry,
I do not brood.
I do not let people,
Dampen my mood.

I laugh out loud,
To chase the gloom.
And take a walk,
To my magic room.

As I slide open,
The magical door.
Life seems different,
Compassionate and pure.

I see sprites flying,
Spraying golden dust.
There's the witch's broom,
Cleaning as it must.

I pick up,
The magic wand.
Swish it once,
Waving my hand.

I try to summon,
The fairy tale folk.
As they apparate,
They dance, sing n talk.

"Here's the key" they say,
To the land of dreams.
Mountains of dark chocolate,
Topped with snowy cream.

Sitting on the silver moon,
Mystical stories I weave.
Oh! I hear the doorbell,
Time for me to leave.

Lyman Frank Baum

"Somewhere over the rainbow, skies are blue, and the dreams that you dare to dream really do come true"

"Somewhere, over the rainbow, way up high, there's a land that I heard of once in a lullaby"

"Imagination has brought mankind through the dark ages to its present state of civilization. Imagination led Columbus to discover America. Imagination led Franklin to discover electricity. Imagination has given us the steam engine, the telephone, the talking-machine, and the automobile, for these things had to be dreamed of before they became realities. So I believe that dreams--daydreams, you know, with your eyes wide open and your brain machinery whizzing--are likely to lead to the betterment of the world. The imaginative child will become the imaginative man or woman most apt to invent, and therefore to foster, civilization."

"And remember, my sentimental friend, that a heart is not judged by how much you love, but by how much you are loved by others"

35

Death of Fireflies

"I gathered my dreams in wisps of silver air,
Wrapped them in pages left them in gods care."

Mother had told me to stay inside,
Our little house next to private drive.
She promised to be back soon enough,
With bread, fruits and other food supplies.

I played with my dolls all day,
Waited and waited for her to return.
The day passed, I felt thirst and hunger,
I even felt my stomach burn.

Then, a loud sound in the adjoining room,
I ran and saw shattered glass on my bed.
I did not panic, as I was almost five,
Though much younger than my brother Fred.

I went in the kitchen avoiding glass,
Remembering what my mother said.

"baby, when hungry look in the right side shelf"
There I found two slices of old bread.

Saw my cat sleeping on the floor,
Gave her a slice from my bread.
She did not even move a muscle,
She was not hungry or..
..was she dead?

I saw the sun sinking below the horizon,
Darkness was approaching once again.
So I caught hold of six fireflies,
To give me company and to illuminate my den.

Morning came but mother did not,
I trotted again towards the kitchen door.
My cat was sleeping in the same position,
So I ate her share lying on the floor.

I decided to go to the refugee camp,
Mother had told me, father was there.
I did not know the way to that place,
But it had to be near, somewhere.

Before I left, I dug a grave for my fireflies,
They were dead and their light had gone.
Then I filled my water bottle to the brim,
For I knew I had to venture out alone.

"As I leave.

God I remind you of my little diary,
Full of unfulfilled dreams lying there.
Please watch over it for me,
As it lies over the topmost stair."

36

God's Words

With his sun gold body and peaceful smile,
Stood The Gold God in front of me.
Dressed in a snowy white silken robe,
Creating an image of felicity.

As he parted his lips to speak,
Silence was filled with sweet melody.
Words spoken took a celestial rhythm,
Opened my mind, set my soul free.
God's words..

"Feel thyself God-born.
Rise beyond thy immortality.
Know thyself limitless,
Timeless, deathless in eternal glory"

37

I, For You..

Why do I lie beneath the old tree,
This is not the place where I should be.

Why aren't you here, O my sweet,
Your absence makes me so incomplete.

Why don't you whisper anymore in my ears,
Tales of our love of yonder years.

Are you upset with me still,
What could I have done against God's will.

At the altar I vowed to be by your side,
Alas with God's wishes I had to abide.

O my love to you I confide,
When I saw death my heart cried.

Six years of being dead still I feel alive,
Because of you even death I survived.

Though I feel scared, for you I try to be brave,
But it hurts, when you don't even visit my grave.

38

His Sonnets and Prose

Look son, at the centre of the ground,
How his statue stands tall and proud.

It was put in the year nineteen seventy,
To honour a poet and his poetry.

Though his statue stays in this posh locality,
Our poet, lived a life of poverty.

Tomorrow they are moving him away,
To another location, they say.

He is being sent back to the slums,
In his native setting, near the garbage dumps.

Tomorrow A Poet will be replaced again,
By another, An important man.

Look son-
He still smiles from those eyes of stone,
Simply, offering us his sonnets and prose.

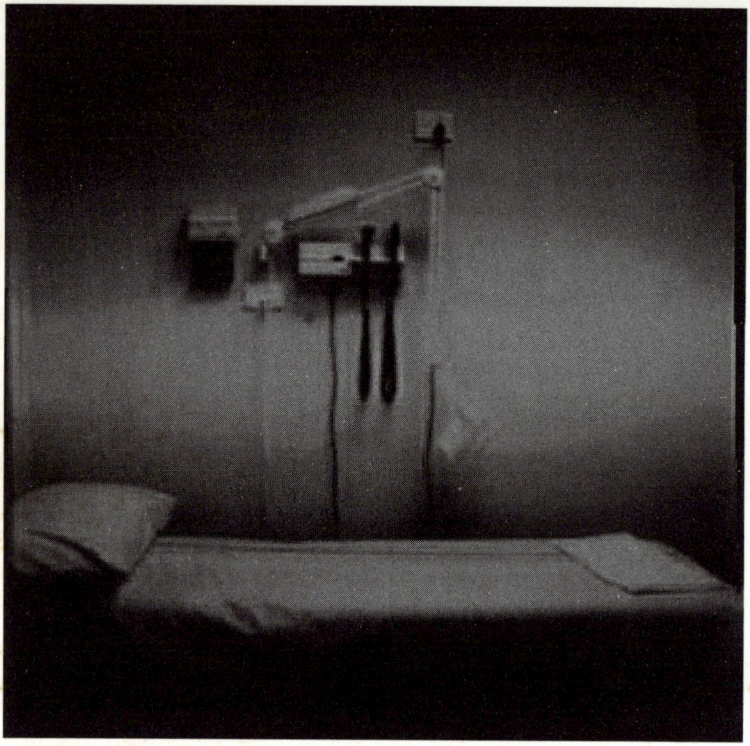

39

As I Sleep

Why this immense silence,
Pierced by the rhythmic beep.
Needles in my flesh,
Medicines which make me sleep.

Am I awake I wonder,
Or is it a semiconscious state.
I can feel my heart surrender,
To death its final fate.

Darkness thinning down now,
I can see the black night fade.
Giving way to the morning sun,
Creating symphony of light and shade.

Talk of death, when life dances,
In my veins goes surging through.
There's still some dawns ahead,
I feel it, it is true.

As I leave this gloomy place,
Get up from my rickety bed.
Fly high above the silver clouds
To see where heaven and earth wed.
I wonder...

Why this immense silence,
Pierced by the rhythmic beep.
People mourning around my body,
While I live on, as I sleep.

W. H. Auden

''Healing,'' Papa would tell me, ''is not a science, but the intuitive art of wooing nature.''

"It is a sad fact about our culture that a poet can earn much more money writing or talking about his art than he can by practicing it."

"Geniuses are the luckiest of mortals because what they must do is the same as what they most want to do."

"A verbal art like poetry is reflective; it stops to think. Music is immediate, it goes on to become."

"A poet is, before anything else, a person who is passionately in love with language.

"A real book is not one that we read, but one that reads us."

"Gravedigger, when you dig my grave, could you make it shallow so that I can feel the rain"

Dave Matthews,
Some Devil